Step-by-Step
Decorative Painting

Judy Balchin

Heinemann Library
Chicago, Illinois

Published by Heinemann Library,
an imprint of Reed Educational & Professional Publishing,
Chicago, IL
Customer Service 888-454-2279
Visit our website at www.heinemannlibrary.com

Originated by Graphics '91, Singapore
Designed by Search Press
Printed in Italy by L.E.G.O.

05 04 03 02 01
10 9 8 7 6 5 4 3 2

Library of Congress Cataloging-in-Publication Data
Balchin, Judy.
   Decorative Painting / Judy Balchin.
      p. cm. -- (Step-by-step)
   Includes bibliographical references and index.
   ISBN 1-57572-330-1 (library binding)
    1. Acrylic painting--Technique--Juvenile literature. 2. Decoration and ornament--Juvenile literature. [1. Handicraft. 2. Painting.] I. Title. II. Step-by-step (Heinemann Library)

  TT385 .B35 2001
  755.7'23--dc21

00-047281

Acknowledgments
The author and publishers are grateful to the following for permission to reproduce copyright material:
Bridgeman Art Library, p.5.

Photographs: Search Press Studios

Every effort has been made to contact copyright holders of any material reproduced in this book. Any omissions will be rectified in subsequent printings if notice is given to the publisher.

**To my daughters Rebecca and Ruth
for being there**

Some words are shown in bold, **like this**. You can find out what they mean by looking in the glossary.

When this sign is used in the book, it means that adult supervision is needed.

REMEMBER!
Ask an adult to help you when you see this sign.

Contents

Introduction

What exactly is meant by decorative painting? Well, let us try to imagine a world where it does not exist—where all surfaces are plain with no decoration. Difficult, isn't it? For thousands of years, people have had an irresistible desire to decorate things, from cave walls and pottery to buildings, furniture, and fabrics. Throughout history people have been attracted to pattern and color, and today you only have to look around your own home or visit your local shopping center to see a wonderful variety of decorative colors and shapes.

Before starting the projects in this book, take a little time to look at the types of decoration used by different civilizations and countries. Each one has its own color preferences and style. This can be seen when you look at floral designs. Flowers have always been popular as a subject, but compare the simple, stylish **Lotus flower** designs of ancient Egyptian artists with the **intricate** blossoms created by the Chinese. Both designs are beautiful, but in different ways.

You do not have to look far to find things to decorate and you do not have to spend a lot of money on them. We use flowers to decorate a box in the following pages, but we also have great fun decorating eggs with monsters, and pebbles with animals. Wooden spoons are decorated with insects, and colorful patchwork squares

are painted on a glass jar to transform it into a fancy candy container.

This book will show you how to paint on different surfaces, including wood, paper, cardboard, **terracotta**, glass, and stone. All the objects can be found easily in or around your home. Cardboard boxes, paper plates, used containers, and many other objects can be transformed with a little paint and some imagination. Acrylic paints are used in every project because they are inexpensive, cover the surface well, and are hard-wearing.

As you work through the projects you will think of other ways of decorating surfaces. Look for unusual things to paint. Be bold with your designs, use bright colors and have lots of fun!

Opposite *Chinese craft workers are famous for their decorated porcelain, which is a form of white pottery. This dog was made in the Seventeenth Century: the unpainted dog would have been fired, or baked, to make it hard before the colorful decoration was applied.*

Materials

The best thing about decorative painting is that it does not cost much to get started. You will not need all the things shown on this page to begin, and you may already have some acrylic paints and brushes. Many of the other materials can be found in your own home. In addition, there are some specific items needed for certain projects, such as an egg cup, plastic eyes, fabric, and ribbons. You should check the list of materials carefully before you start each project.

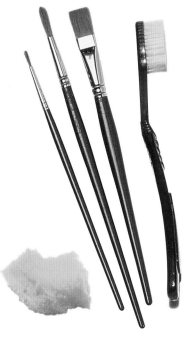

It is possible to paint on all sorts of things and all kinds of surfaces with acrylic paints. *Paper* and *cardboard* are ideal, but so are **terracotta** and *glass.* You can also paint on *eggshell, pebbles,* and *wood.*

Paints can be applied with *paintbrushes.* An assortment of sizes are used in this book. A piece of *sponge* can also be used to apply paint. Interesting effects can be created with a *toothbrush*—this is used for splattering paint.

Acrylic paint is used for the projects in this book. These paints can normally be used straight from their tubes, but it is best to use paint from a **palette** when you are sponging color on a surface. *Varnish* can also be used to give a shiny appearance.

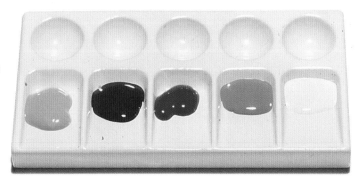

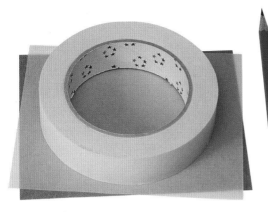

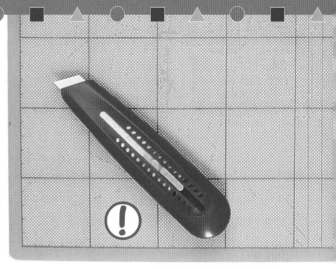

Tracing paper, **carbon paper** and a *pencil* are used to transfer designs. *Masking tape* should be used to hold the designs in place. This can also mask areas when painting and secure loops of string to the back of projects.

A *craft knife* is used to cut plastic or thick cardboard. Always ask an adult to do this for you as craft knifes are very sharp. Craft knives should be used on a *cutting mat*.

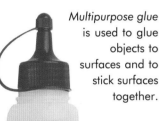

Multipurpose glue is used to glue objects to surfaces and to stick surfaces together.

Scissors are used to cut paper, posterboard, and string.

String is ideal for making hanging loops which are secured to the back of projects.

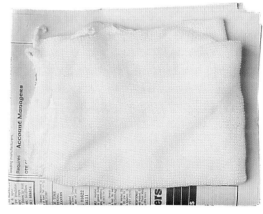

Sheets of *newspaper* can be used to cover your work surface. An old *cloth* provides a stable base for a curved object that requires painting.

Thin cardboard (for example, from a cereal box) or *thick cardboard* are ideal as a base for a project. *Mirror cardboard* can be used if you want to make a fun mirror.

Techniques

Decorative painting is not difficult to do, but it is worth reading through this section carefully before you start. The techniques are demonstrated on a cardboard box. Always clean brushes thoroughly in water after using them.

Note Decorative painting can be messy so it is best to cover your work surface with a large piece of newspaper.

Painting

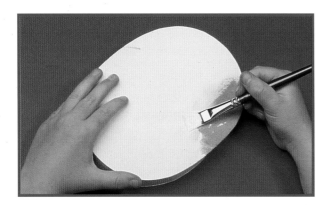

Use a flat brush to paint large surfaces. This gives an even finish which is easier to work on. Sometimes, you may need to apply two coats of paint so the surface is well covered. Allow the first coat to dry before applying the second.

Splattering

Protect the work surface with newspaper. Dilute some paint on a **palette** with water so that it is runny. Dip the bristles of a toothbrush in the paint. Hold the toothbrush with the bristles towards the surface you are decorating and run your finger along the brush. This will splatter random paint spots onto the surface.

Masking and sponging

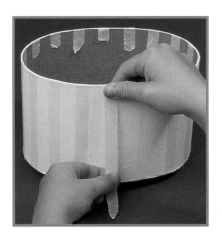

To mask areas of an object, press strips of masking tape onto the surface. Make sure that the edges of the tape are smoothed flat. The masked areas will remain the base color.

When sponging, pour a little paint onto a palette. Dip the sponge in the paint, and then dab the surfaces all over. Remove the masking tape to reveal neat stripes.

Stenciling, painting, and outlining

Now that the surfaces have been prepared with flat color and textured effects, images can be added. Stencils are a quick and easy way to create pictures that can be added to and outlined.

1 Tape the stencil to the surface with small pieces of masking tape. Use a sponge to dab the paint through the stencil. Remove the stencil.

2 Paint in the pattern using a small paintbrush. Pull the brush towards you smoothly, lifting it off the surface as you complete the stroke to create a neat brush line.

3 Outlining with black paint makes images really stand out. For this design, use a small round paintbrush to outline the leaves and the left-hand side of the grapes. This will create a **three-dimensional** effect.

Bumble Bee Spoon

The insect world is fascinating and amazing. Think of the bee, the ladybug, and the butterfly—they are all so different. Their amazing range of shapes and colors is not accidental. Insects use their colors and patterns as a defense against enemies and to attract other insects. In this project a bee motif is used to decorate a wooden spoon, and the same colors are used on the handle. Wood is a wonderfully smooth surface to paint on. If your spoon is a little rough, sand it down with sandpaper before starting.

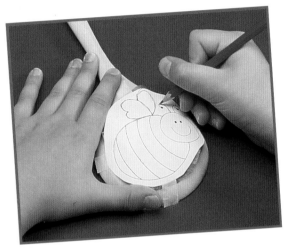

1 **Transfer** the pattern on page 29 onto the back of the spoon following the instructions on page 28.

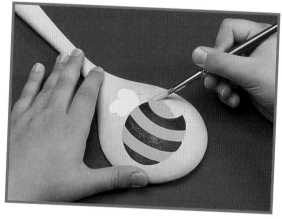

2 Paint the black stripes and then paint the bee's body and head using a small paintbrush and a light color. Let the paint dry.

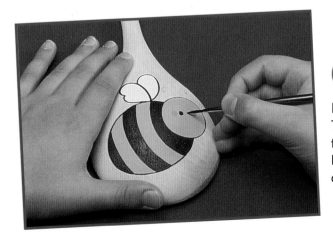

3 Paint the bee's cheeks. Then carefully outline the bee in a dark color. Paint in the eyes, mouth, and antennae.

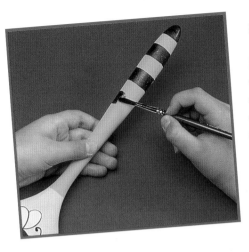

Paint the handle with the lighter color. When it is dry, paint the darker stripes.

Use a larger paintbrush to varnish the back of the spoon. When the varnish is dry, turn the spoon over and varnish the front.

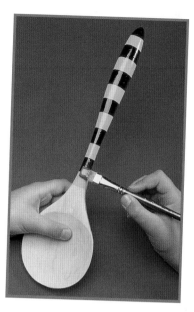

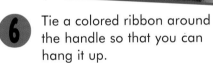

6 Tie a colored ribbon around the handle so that you can hang it up.

Note This bumble bee spoon is purely decorative and should not be used to cook or eat with.

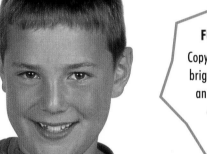

FURTHER IDEAS
Copy paintings of other brightly colored insects and make your own colony of insect spoons.

Rosy Gift Box

Artists have painted and decorated surfaces with flowers for a long time, inspired by the beautiful colors and shapes they have found in nature. Many fine examples of flower paintings can be found in museums and art galleries. These simple roses are easy to paint. They are used to transform a plain cardboard container into a lovely gift box. Look for an old box to decorate—you do not have to buy one.

YOU WILL NEED
Cardboard box
Black acrylic paint
Colored acrylic paint
Large and small paintbrushes
Sponge • **Palette**

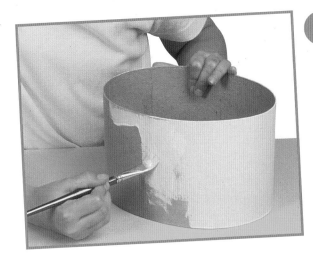

1 Use a large brush to paint the box and lid with a pale color. You may need to apply two coats if the first one does not cover the surface completely. Make sure that the first coat is dry before applying the second.

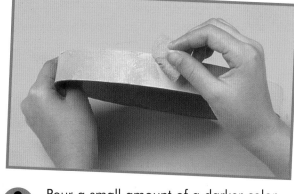

2 Pour a small amount of a darker color into a palette. Dip the sponge in the paint and dab it around the base and rim of the lid. Let the paint dry.

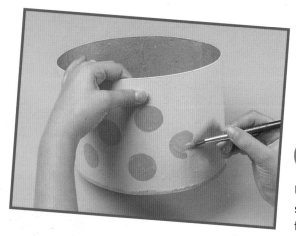

3 Using a smaller brush and the same color, paint circles all over the lid and box. Let the paint dry.

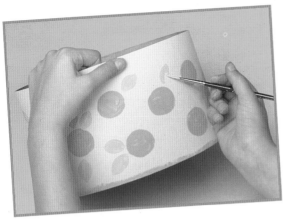

 4 Paint leaf shapes around the circles using a different color. Try to fill in any gaps. Let the paint dry.

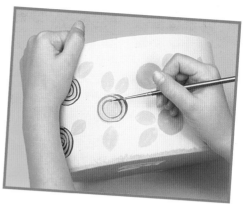

 5 Decorate each colored circle with a large swirl using black paint and a small paintbrush. Allow the paint to dry.

 6 Outline the leaves with black paint and add a vein line down the center of each one.

FURTHER IDEAS

Decorate boxes with different flowers—daisies, sunflowers, and poppies for example. Keep the designs simple, and use bright colors.

Sun Wall Hanging

Astronomy is the study of the sun, moon, planets, and stars. Astronomical symbols have been used as decoration by many artists throughout the ages. The sun is ninety-three million miles away from Earth, but you can bring it right into your own home by creating this colorful sun wall hanging. A paper plate is the perfect round surface on which to work. The basic design is painted and then decorated with dots and swirls of metallic paint.

YOU WILL NEED
Paper plate
Colored and metallic acrylic paint
Large and small paintbrushes
Tracing paper • **Carbon paper**
Masking tape • Pencil
Scissors • String

Note Place your plate over a roll of masking tape. This will help support the plate when you are painting it.

Using a large paintbrush, paint the center of the plate in a light color and the border in a dark color. Let the paint dry.

Transfer the pattern on page 29 to the center of the plate, following the instructions on page 28. Using a small paintbrush, outline the features in a dark color and paint the eyes and cheeks. Let the paint dry.

Paint the eyebrows, eyelids, lips, and chin with a lighter color. Allow the paint to dry.

 4 Use a pencil to draw the sun's rays around the border. Carefully cut them out.

5 Decorate the sun's face with dotted swirls of metallic paint. Add dotted swirls to the rays. Let the paint dry.

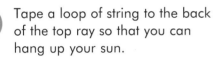

 6 Tape a loop of string to the back of the top ray so that you can hang up your sun.

FURTHER IDEAS

Make moon and star wall hangings to **complement** your sun—or decorate lots of small plates and create a matching mobile.

Patchwork Candy Jar

For generations, people have created patchwork using scraps and odd remnants of material. You may have seen beautifully stitched quilts made in this way. They are usually made to **commemorate** an event or special occasion, such as a wedding. In this project you will use paint to create your own patchwork. An old glass jar is decorated and transformed into a stylish candy container. Look for a large jar to show off your painting. Do not forget to wash and dry it thoroughly before you begin.

YOU WILL NEED
Large glass jar
Black and white acrylic paint
Colored acrylic paint
Large and small paintbrushes
Pencil • Varnish • Candy
Colored fabric • Scissors
Rubber band
Colored ribbon

 Paint the jar with two coats of white paint using a large brush. Leave an unpainted square in the middle, so when the jar is finished you can see what is in it. Let the first coat of paint dry before applying the second coat.

 Use a pencil to divide the jar up into squares.

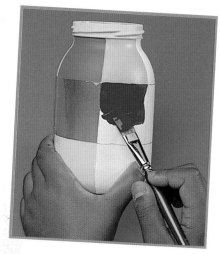

 Paint the neck of the jar using a large paintbrush and a bright color. When the paint is dry, paint in the squares using different colors. Let the paint dry.

5

Add stitch lines around each square using a small paintbrush and black paint. Let the paint dry and then, using a large brush, apply a coat of varnish to the jar.

4 Decorate each square with dots, lines, or hearts. Try to make each square different.

FURTHER IDEAS
Recycle old bottles and create colorful patchwork patterns on them— or decorate other glass objects.

6 Fill the jar with candy. Cut out a circle of fabric double the size of the top of the jar. Secure the fabric around the top with a rubber band. Finally, tie a ribbon over the rubber band.

Padlocked Money Box

This project uses *trompe l'oeil*, a French term that means "fool the eye." It refers to something that looks real, but is not—it is just an **illusion**. The padlock and chain on this money box look real, but they are just painted on. Painted shadow lines and highlights make them look **three-dimensional**.

 Paint the cardboard tube with white paint using a large brush and allow the paint to dry. You may have to apply a few coats of paint to cover any lettering. Wait for the last coat to dry and then apply two coats of metallic paint.

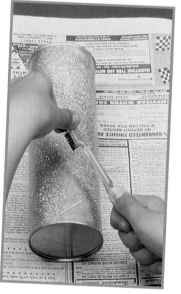

2 Cover your work surface with sheets of newspaper. Lay the tube on top. Pour small amounts of black and white paint into a **palette** and dilute them both with water. Using a toothbrush and following the instructions on page 8, splatter the tube first with white, then with black paint. Roll the tube to make sure that you splatter the whole surface.

3 Follow the instructions on page 8 to **transfer** the pattern on page 30 to the tube and fill it in with metallic paint. Let the paint dry.

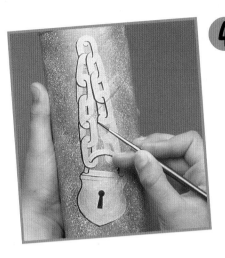

4 Using a small paintbrush, paint the keyhole. Add black shadow lines down the left-hand side and along the bottom of the chain links and padlock. Let the paint dry.

5 Create highlights by painting white lines down the right-hand side and along the tops of the chain links and padlock.

6 Cut a slot in the top of the lid with a craft knife and place the lid on top of the tube.

(!) A craft knife is very sharp; it should always be used with a cutting mat. Ask an adult to help you.

FURTHER IDEAS

Design some symbols that mean "Keep out," "Private," "Danger" and use these to decorate your money box.

Tiger Paperweight

Decorating pebbles or stones is an unusual and fascinating craft, and it is easy to do. Part of the fun is finding just the right shape. Find a stone that suggests the shape of a tiger, and make sure that it has a smooth surface so it will be easier to paint on. Keep your design simple and use bold colors for the best effect.

YOU WILL NEED
Stone
White and black acrylic paint
Colored acrylic paint
Large and small paintbrushes
Pencil • Two plastic eyes
Multipurpose glue

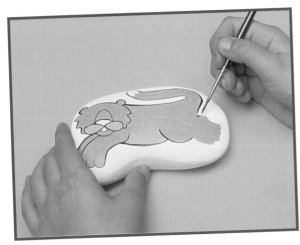

1 Paint the stone white using a large paintbrush. Let the paint dry. Copy the pattern from page 30 onto the stone using a pencil.

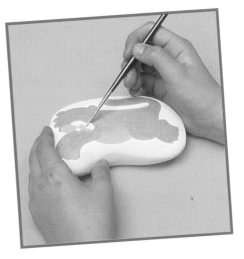

2 Using an appropriate color, paint in the darker areas of the body, and then paint in the lighter areas.

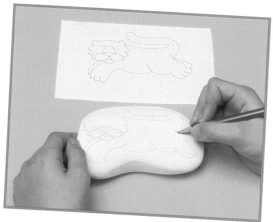

3 Outline the tiger using a small paintbrush and black paint.

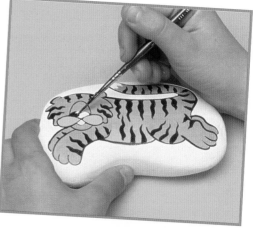

4 Add the stripes, nose, and mouth using a small paintbrush and black paint. Let the paint dry.

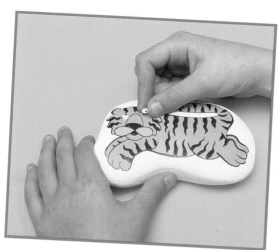

5 Glue the plastic eyes to the stone and let the glue dry.

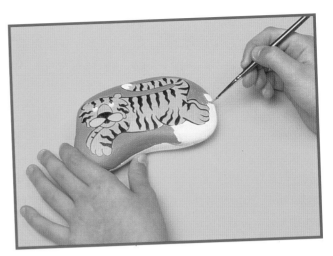

6 Paint the rest of the stone in a bright color. Let the paint dry.

FURTHER IDEAS
Look for stones with unusual shapes and create your own animals and birds.

Fruity Flower Pot

Artists and craft workers often use fruit motifs as decoration because of the amazing variety of shapes and colors they offer. Try making a list of all the fruits you can think of and you will soon realize what a wonderful choice there is—oranges, apples, strawberries, lemons, grapes, and more! This fruity project combines masking with sponging and stenciling—easy techniques that transform a plain **terracotta** pot into a colorful decorative plant container. Use an inexpensive sponge and tear pieces off as you need them.

 Paint the pot in a light color using a large paintbrush. Let the paint dry. Apply vertical strips of masking tape around the pot as shown on page 8. Try to make the gaps between the strips the same.

2 Pour some darker colored paint into a **palette** and sponge the unmasked stripes, following the instructions on page 8. Carefully remove the masking tape and let the paint dry.

3 Carefully sponge the top of the rim and the base of the pot with a different color.

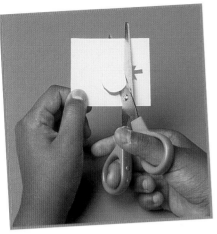

5

Lay the pot down on an old cloth to keep it from rolling around. Tape the stencil to the pot with masking tape.

4 **Transfer** the strawberry pattern on page 29 to thin cardboard. Cut out the strawberry shape to create a stencil.

6 Sponge paint through the stencil onto the pot. Choose two appropriate colors and use two pieces of sponge to color the top of the strawberry and then the fruit. Work around the pot varying the angle of the strawberries.

FURTHER IDEAS

Change your designs by painting horizontal stripes around your pot and choose other types of fruit.

Monster Egg

An artist named Carl Fabergé created beautifully decorated eggs in the late nineteenth century. Some of his more precious jeweled eggs were made for the Russian royal family. You can use a hard boiled egg for this project and create an optical illusion. Although the monster is painted on the surface of the egg, it looks as though he is living inside it! If you want projects to last a long time, **polystyrene,** or **papier mâché** eggs can be decorated using the same techniques.

(!) Ask an adult to boil the egg for you before you start the project.

1 Paint the top half of the egg in a color of your choice using a large paintbrush. Sit it in an egg cup and let the paint dry. Turn it over and paint the bottom half. Let the paint dry. Be careful not to get paint on the egg cup.

2 Using a pencil, copy the monster pattern from page 30 onto the egg.

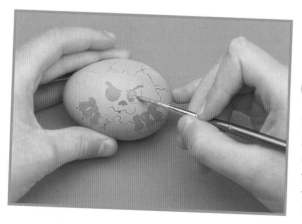

3 Paint the fingers using a brighter color. Mix a touch of black with this color to darken it and paint in the nose and eyes with a small paintbrush. The darker color will make it look as though the monster is hiding in a shadowy hole.

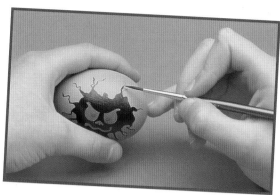

4 Add the claws, mouth, and staring eyes using another bright color.

5 Fill in the area behind the monster's features using black paint. Outline the fingers with the same paint, and then add the lines around the edge of the hole.

Paint a thin white line along one side and along the bottom of the hole. Paint small white dots at the base of the fingers. This gives the appearance of highlights which makes the monster look even more **three-dimensional**.

6

FURTHER IDEAS
Use metallic acrylic paints to create realistic alien eggs or invent your own monster.

Picasso Mirror

This project is inspired by the work of the Spanish artist, Pablo Picasso. He was born in 1881 and was one of the greatest painters of the twentieth century. You can use the style and colors of his work to create your own masterpiece.

YOU WILL NEED

Thick cardboard
Colored acrylic paint
Black acrylic paint
Small paintbrush • Tracing paper
Carbon paper • Masking tape
Pencil • Craft knife • Scissors
Cutting mat • Mirror cardboard
Multipurpose glue
String

 1

Follow the instructions on page 28 to **transfer** the pattern from page 31 to cardboard. Using bright colors and a small paintbrush, start filling in the design.

 3

Outline the design using black paint. Let the paint dry. Cut off the outer unpainted border using a craft knife. Cut out the unpainted central section.

!

A craft knife is very sharp and it should always be used with a cutting mat. Make sure you ask an adult to help you when you use it.

2 Continue painting the frame until all the areas are filled in.

 4

Paint the outside and inside edges of the cut cardboard black.

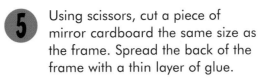

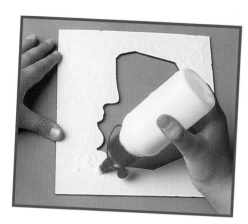

5 Using scissors, cut a piece of mirror cardboard the same size as the frame. Spread the back of the frame with a thin layer of glue.

6

Carefully press the frame down onto the mirror cardboard, matching all the corners. Let the glue dry.

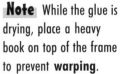 While the glue is drying, place a heavy book on top of the frame to prevent **warping**.

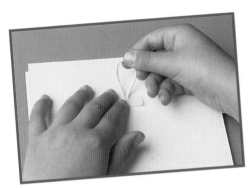

7 Tape a loop of string to the back of the frame with masking tape so that you can hang up your mirror.

FURTHER IDEAS

Look at the work of other famous artists. Decorate picture frames or mirror frames in their styles.

Patterns

You can trace the patterns on these pages straight from the book as shown in step 1. You can also make them larger on a photocopier, and then follow steps 2–4.

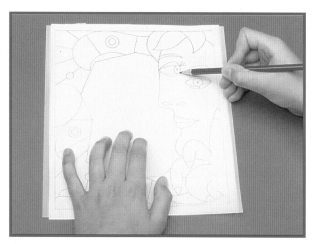

1 Place a piece of tracing paper over the pattern and tape it down with small pieces of masking tape. Trace around the outlines using a soft pencil.

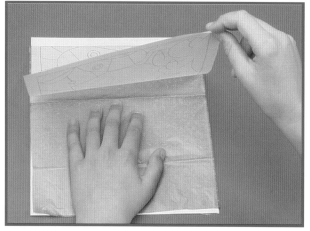

2 Place the tracing paper or photocopy on the surface of the project and tape it at the top. Slide a sheet of **carbon paper** underneath and tape it at the bottom.

3 Trace over the outlines with the pencil, pressing down firmly.

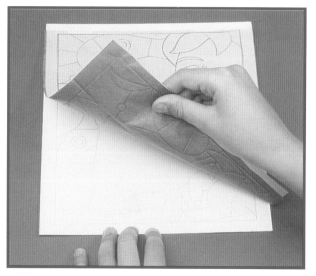

4 Remove the tracing paper and the carbon paper to reveal the design.

This pattern is for the
Fruity Flower Pot featured
on pages 22–23.

This pattern is for
the Bumble Bee
Spoon featured on
pages 10–11

This pattern is for the Sun Wall Hanging
featured on pages 14–15.

This pattern is for the Monster Egg featured on pages 24–25.

This pattern is for the Padlocked Money Box featured on pages 18–19.

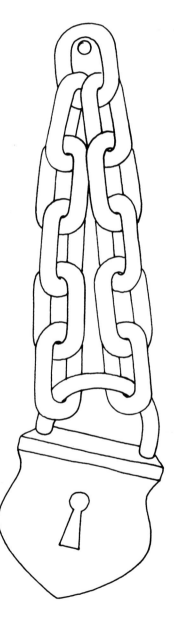

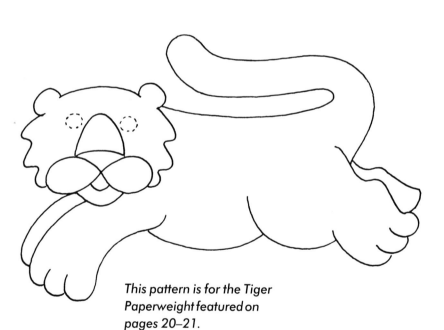

This pattern is for the Tiger Paperweight featured on pages 20–21.

This pattern is for the Picasso Mirror featured on pages 26–27.

Glossary

Astronomy   science that deals with the study of the universe outside of Earth's atmosphere

Carbon paper   paper with a dark coating that is placed between two pieces of plain paper so that pencil marks on the top piece of paper go through to the second piece

Commemorate   to honor the memory of an event or person

Complement   to add to or highlight

Illusion   something that seems to be real but is not

Intricate   having many parts or details

Lotus Flower   water lily

Palette   thin wooden board or plastic dish used to hold and mix different colours of paint

Papier Mâché   art material created with strips of paper soaked in liquid paste that harden as they dry

Polystyrene   stiff plastic foam often used for cups for hot liquids such as coffee and hot chocolate

Terracotta   "cooked earth"; orange-colored clay formed into pots or other containers and baked until hard and dry

Three-dimensional   seeming to have width, height, and depth; appearing real and solid

Transfer   to move something from one place to another

Warp   to become bent or twisted out of shape

More Books to Read

Bower, Jane. *Painting*. Danbury, Conn.: Children's Press, 1998.

Foster, P. *Painting*. Tulsa, Okla.: E D C Publishing, 1999. An older reader can help you with this book.

Gibson, R., and R. Gee. *Paint Fun*. Tulsa, Okla.: E D C Publishing, 1999.

Index